EVOLVE

WORKBOOK

Mari Vargo

6A

CAMBRIDGE
UNIVERSITY PRESS

University Printing House, Cambridge CB2 8BS, United Kingdom

One Liberty Plaza, 20th Floor, New York, NY 10006, USA

477 Williamstown Road, Port Melbourne, VIC 3207, Australia

314–321, 3rd Floor, Plot 3, Splendor Forum, Jasola District Centre, New Delhi – 110025, India

103 Penang Road, #05-06/07, Visioncrest Commercial, Singapore 238467

Cambridge University Press is part of the University of Cambridge.

It furthers the University's mission by disseminating knowledge in the pursuit of education, learning and research at the highest international levels of excellence.

www.cambridge.org
Information on this title: www.cambridge.org/9781108408851

© Cambridge University Press 2020

First published 2020

20 19 18 17 16 15 14 13 12 11 10 9 8 7 6 5 4 3 2

Printed in Great Britain by CPI Group (UK) Ltd, Croydon CR0 4YY

A catalogue record for this publication is available from the British Library

ISBN 978-1-108-40535-5 Student's Book
ISBN 978-1-108-40514-0 Student's Book A
ISBN 978-1-108-40931-5 Student's Book B
ISBN 978-1-108-40537-9 Student's Book with Practice Extra
ISBN 978-1-108-40515-7 Student's Book with Practice Extra A
ISBN 978-1-108-40932-2 Student's Book with Practice Extra B
ISBN 978-1-108-40909-4 Workbook with Audio
ISBN 978-1-108-40885-1 Workbook with Audio A
ISBN 978-1-108-41196-7 Workbook with Audio B
ISBN 978-1-108-40520-1 Teacher's Edition with Test Generator
ISBN 978-1-108-41077-9 Presentation Plus
ISBN 978-1-108-41206-3 Class Audio CDs
ISBN 978-1-108-40802-8 Video Resource Book with DVD
ISBN 978-1-108-41451-7 Full Contact with DVD
ISBN 978-1-108-41157-8 Full Contact with DVD A
ISBN 978-1-108-41424-1 Full Contact with DVD B

Additional resources for this publication at www.cambridge.org/evolve

CONTENTS

1 ROBOT REVOLUTION 2

2 THE LABELS WE LIVE BY 10

3 IN HINDSIGHT 18

4 CLOSE UP 26

5 REMOTE 34

6 SURPRISE, SURPRISE 42

Extra activities 98

UNIT 1 ROBOT REVOLUTION

1.1 THE ROBOT TOUCH

1 VOCABULARY: Using adverbs to add detail

A **Match the adverbs with the definitions.**

1	comprehensively	_c_	**a**	certain to happen
2	ultimately		**b**	definitely
3	demonstrably		**c**	in a complete way
4	inevitably		**d**	little by little; in a gradual way
5	drastically		**e**	in the end
6	progressively		**f**	in a reasonable way
7	undoubtedly		**g**	in a way that can be shown or proven
8	feasibly		**h**	in an extreme way

B **Find the words.**

dramatically	gradually	increasingly	markedly	potentially	radically	unquestionably

R	A	T	P	O	K	G	F	D	C	U	I	A	P	R	C
E	K	S	O	J	E	S	M	V	T	K	X	N	N	A	P
U	N	Q	U	E	S	T	I	O	N	A	B	L	Y	D	O
T	R	Y	G	H	G	K	Q	U	S	I	E	Q	P	I	T
P	N	I	L	Y	R	C	P	N	H	N	L	L	Y	C	E
I	N	C	R	E	A	S	I	N	G	L	Y	G	K	A	N
L	Y	M	S	M	D	G	L	D	I	C	R	A	J	L	T
Y	K	T	S	M	U	U	Y	V	N	M	P	E	S	L	I
C	G	M	D	R	A	M	A	T	I	C	A	L	L	Y	A
I	R	L	L	Y	L	R	I	F	L	H	K	O	T	B	L
E	K	I	O	T	L	K	D	U	Y	C	R	L	L	Y	L
G	P	S	D	N	Y	C	Z	M	A	R	K	E	D	L	Y

2 GRAMMAR: Commenting adverbs with future forms

A **Put the words in the correct order to make sentences.**

1 part / lives in / robots will / of our / a big / inevitably / be / the future / .
   Robots will inevitably be a big part of our lives in the future.

2 many / potentially / they are / types / take over / different / going to / of jobs / .

3 able / some / certainly / not be / jobs / they will / to do / .

4 progressively / more dependent / on robots / however, we / become / will / .

3 GRAMMAR AND VOCABULARY

A **Write sentences about the future using the word prompts and a commenting adverb.**

1 Some people believe / robots / look more human

   Some people believe robots will gradually look more human.

2 They / move and talk more like us

   _____

3 Robots / become involved in our personal lives

   _____

4 According to some people, we / develop relationships with robots

   _____

5 We / have robots as our friends and coworkers

   _____

6 Robots / make our lives easier.

   _____

7 Having robots around / improve our quality of life.

   _____

8 It / be impossible to tell the difference between robots and humans

   _____

B **How do you think life will be different with robots? Complete the sentences with the commenting adverbs in parentheses and your own ideas.**

1 Every home (ultimately) _____

   _____

2 Robots (increasingly) _____

   _____

3 Hospitals (potentially) _____

   _____

4 Robots (drastically) _____

   _____

5 Cities (inevitably) _____

   _____

1 VOCABULARY: Talking about developments in technology

A **Complete the conversations with words from the boxes.**

Conversation 1

~~artificial intelligence~~	beta version	chatbots
facial recognition	virtual assistants	voice activation
working prototype		

Pia   What are you reading, Sam?

Sam   I'm reading an article about AI.

Pia   What's AI?

Sam   It stands for [1] _____artificial intelligence_____ . This company is developing [2] _____ to talk to their customers online. So far, they have developed a [3] _____ . This early version still has a lot of problems. They think their [4] _____ will be ready in a couple of years.

Pia   That's interesting. Are they only going to use it for customer service?

Sam   Well, right now the company is using simpler chatbots as [5] _____ . These devices use [6] _____ , so you just talk to them to turn them on. They also have cameras and use [7] _____ , so when you look at them, they know who you are.

Conversation 2

computer-generated speech	computer translation	image recognition
operating system	text to speech	voice recognition

Carlo   Hey, Allie, what are you doing?

Allie   I'm getting ready for my trip to Italy. I'm downloading a new app. It's a [8] _____ app because I don't speak much Italian.

Carlo   Cool. Is it easy to use?

Allie   It's really easy to use. You just say something in English. The computer uses [9] _____ , so it understands what you say and shows you the Italian translation. It also uses [10] _____ , so your phone can say the words after translating them.

Carlo   That's cool. Does it sound like a real person, or does it sound like really bad [11] _____ ?

Allie   It sounds like a real person. It uses [12] _____ , too, so you can take a photo of text and the phone can translate the text from the picture.

Carlo   I could really use that. I wonder if it would work with my [13] _____ .

Allie   It should work on any phone or tablet. You should try it!

2 GRAMMAR: Future perfect and future continuous

A **Find the errors and rewrite each sentence.**

1 I'll staying at my sister's house next week.

_____

2 We'll have finish dinner before the movie starts.

_____

3 I have taken eight classes by the end of the year.

_____

4 You be working with Kim on this project.

_____

5 Everyone will leave by the time Mark gets here.

_____

B (Circle) **the correct phrases to complete the conversation.**

Pedro Are you excited about your trip?

Yuki Yes, I am! Tomorrow morning, ¹(*I'll be driving*)/ *I'll have driven* to my friend Tina's house by the beach.

Pedro Have you been there before?

Yuki No, I haven't, so ²*I'll be using / I'll have used the* GPS to find her house.

Pedro ³*Will you be studying / Will you have studied* while you're there?

Yuki No, ⁴*I'll be finishing / I'll have finished* all my schoolwork, so ⁵*I'll be relaxing / I'll have relaxed* on the beach.

Pedro Is anyone else going to be there with you?

Yuki Yes, our friend Sarah is also coming. She's leaving tonight, so ⁶*she'll be arriving / she'll have arrived* by the time I get there.

Pedro ⁷*How long will you be staying / How long will you have stayed*?

Yuki I'll be there for a week. I can't wait! ⁸*We'll be talking and having fun / We'll have talked and had fun* all week long.

3 GRAMMAR AND VOCABULARY

A **Answer the questions with your own ideas about developments in technology. Write complete sentences.**

1 In twenty years, what new technology do you think will be available that we don't have now?

_____

2 What technology will have disappeared?

_____

3 What technology will we be using all the time?

_____

4 What things will we still be able to do without technology?

_____

1.3 I GET WHAT YOU'RE SAYING …

1 LISTENING

A **🔊 1.01 LISTEN FOR ATTITUDE** Listen to a conversation between two friends, Carrie and Paul. Answer the questions.

1 Does Carrie like the app or not?

_____

2 What does Carrie say that shows how she feels about the app?

_____

3 Does Paul like the app or not?

_____

4 What does Paul say that shows how he feels about the app?

_____

B **🔊 1.01 LISTEN FOR MAIN POINTS** Listen again. Complete the chart with positives and negatives of facial recognition technology.

Positives	Negatives

2 CRITICAL THINKING

A **THINK CRITICALLY** Who do you think would want to use facial recognition technology? Who do you think would not want to use it? Explain your ideas.

_____

_____

_____

_____

3 SPEAKING

A **Complete the conversations with the phrases in the box. Two of the phrases won't be used.**

can see how	good point there	guess so	look at it that way
really thought of it	valid point	~~you're coming from~~	you're saying

1 A Robots have advanced so much in the past few years. I think they'll drastically change the way we live in the next five years or so.

   B I get where _____*you're coming from*_____, but I don't think things will change that radically.

2 A I don't like to use virtual assistants. I've heard that everything they hear is recorded and stored. I don't want all of my personal conversations recorded.

   B I hadn't _____ like that. Now I don't know if I want to keep mine.

3 A I hope chatbots don't replace all customer service personnel. I like talking to real people.

   B I understand what _____, but I think chatbots will help companies save money, and then their goods and services will be cheaper to buy.

4 A I don't think we should let robots do so many different jobs. They'll take jobs away from people.

   B You could _____, but if robots do simple jobs, humans will be able to do more interesting work.

5 A Language is really complex. Computer translation apps make so many mistakes. That's why I don't like to use them.

   B That's a _____, but they can be helpful sometimes.

6 A I think I would feel uncomfortable having a robot that looks like a human cooking, cleaning, and walking around in my home. It would be weird.

   B I _____, but it would be really convenient not to have to cook and clean anymore.

B **Write a conversation for each situation. Use the language you practiced in exercise 3A.**

1 Anna doesn't like using speech-to-text because there are always so many mistakes. Timo thinks it saves time and helps people who have trouble with their hands.

Anna _____

Timo _____

Anna _____

Timo _____

2 Michael thinks that everyone should study technology instead of art or literature because technology will be more important in the future. Mila thinks that studying art and literature make us think creatively, and that will help us develop better technology.

Michael _____

Mila _____

Michael _____

Mila _____

1 READING

A **PREDICT CONTENT FROM PICTURES** Look at the pictures. What ideas do you think might be explored in this essay? Check (✓) the ideas. Then read the essay and check your answers.

a benefits of computer translation ☐

b advantages of speaking multiple languages ☐

c what human translators do better than computers ☐

d disadvantages of computer translation ☐

e costs of human translators vs. computers ☐

● ● ● ◁ ▷   🔍 🏠

ROBOT TRANSLATORS – THEY'RE FASTER, BUT ARE THEY BETTER?

Robots have already become a necessity in some industries. For instance, automobile factories rely on car-building robots for their precision and speed. The mining industry uses robots to mine efficiently and safely. Robotics technology will undoubtedly continue to advance, and robots will be replacing humans in a variety of fields. However, in the field of translation, artificial intelligence is no match for humans.

Computerized translation has its benefits. In situations such as, government meetings and international conferences, computers can translate for hours on end without tiring, unlike human translators. While a person can type an average of about 40 words per minute, a computer can work more than ten times as fast. In addition, a single computer can translate an unlimited number of languages. A person can only translate one language at a time.

Despite the benefits of computer technology, humans will likely always produce better and more accurate translations. First of all, no computer can understand all the slang, idioms, expressions, and local variations in even a single language. For example, how would a robot translate the expression "I've got your back," which does not translate literally? Second, computers can't pick up on things like the subtle differences in the meanings of words, tone, emotion, humor, or sarcasm. For instance, would a robot understand the slang usage of the phrase "give me a ring," which can mean "call me"? Third, language constantly changes. New words are born and existing words take on new meanings. All of these factors can lead to mistranslations and confusion. For these reasons, it will probably be a long time before computers can feasibly replace humans in the field of translation.

B **READ FOR DETAIL** Read the essay again. Answer the questions.

1 What reasons does the writer give for stating that computer translation technology is not as good as human translators?

_____

_____

2 According to the writer, what are some benefits of computerized translation?

_____

_____

2 CRITICAL THINKING

A **THINK CRITICALLY** Answer the question.

Do you think someone who speaks multiple languages would agree or disagree with this essay? Explain.

_____

_____

A (Circle) the correct expressions.

1 In the field of medicine, robots perform a variety of tasks, *just to name a few /* (*such as*) dispensing medicine and assisting in surgeries.

2 We're already using robots in our daily lives. *To name a few, / Take, for example,* chatbots.

3 Robots can do things humans can't—lift heavy objects, make extremely fast calculations, and work for 24 hours straight, *just to name a few / namely.*

4 I would love to have a robot in my house to do a lot of things I don't want to do, *like / take, for example,* wash the dishes and clean the bathroom.

5 Many households already use robot technology for housekeeping purposes. *Namely / For instance,* robotic vacuum cleaners are very popular.

B **You are going to write an essay in response to the statement below. Do you agree or disagree with the statement? Organize your ideas in an outline for a three-paragraph essay. Then write your essay.**

Future advances in technology are going to give us more free time.

Paragraph 1: Discussing the statement and its potential consequences _____

_____

_____

Paragraph 2: Exploring counterarguments _____

_____

_____

Paragraph 3: Giving a personal opinion _____

_____

_____

CHECK AND REVIEW

Read the statements. Can you do these things?

UNIT 1	Mark the boxes. ☑ I can do it. ？ I am not sure.		If you are not sure, go back to these pages in the Student's Book.
	I can ...		
VOCABULARY	☐	use adverbs to add detail.	page 2
	☐	use words about developments in technology.	page 4
GRAMMAR	☐	use commenting adverbs with future forms.	page 3
	☐	use future perfect and future continuous.	page 5
LISTENING AND SPEAKING SKILLS	☐	listen for attitude in a conversation.	page 6
	☐	acknowledge arguments and propose counterarguments.	page 7
READING AND WRITING SKILLS	☐	read for detail in an article.	page 8
	☐	write an essay about future advances in technology.	page 9

2.1   IS THAT REALLY ME?

1   VOCABULARY: Describing personality

A   **Complete the sentences. Match 1–6 with a–f.**

1 Someone who likes to talk a lot is …	_d_	**a** aloof.
2 Someone who is trustworthy and genuine is …	....	**b** narrow-minded.
3 Someone who doesn't accept new or different ideas is …	....	**c** self-centered.
4 Someone who doesn't seem affected by anything is …	....	**d** chatty.
5 Someone who likes to learn about new ideas and try new things is …	....	**e** sincere.
6 Someone who talks only about themselves in conversations is …	....	**f** open-minded.

B   **Cross out the word that doesn't belong.**

1	chatty	~~quiet~~	talkative
2	fake	sincere	genuine
3	unfriendly	open-minded	aloof
4	self-centered	selfish	generous
5	rigid	narrow-minded	accepting
6	insensitive	friendly	selfish
7	aloof	antisocial	chatty

C   **Complete the sentences with words from the box.**

~~aloof~~	chatty	narrow-minded	open-minded	self-centered	sincere

1   People often think I'm _____aloof_____ because I don't talk very much.

2   It's difficult to talk about new ideas with _____ people.
    They have a hard time understanding things that they aren't familiar with.

3   John is so _____. He only thinks about himself.

4   If Alice tells you that she likes something, you can believe her.
    She's always very _____ .

5   I'm trying to be more _____
    and accept people the way they are.

6   I like Andrew, but he is so

    _____ .

    Sometimes I just need quiet time.

2 GRAMMAR: Uses of *will*

A **Read the assumptions or deductions below. Are they about the past or the present?**

1 If it's noon, Marco will not have have eaten lunch yet.   past

2 Tomas will do every personality quiz he finds online.   _____

3 James will usually be on social media in the mornings.   _____

4 Karen will have posted all of these photos on social media by the end of the day.   _____

5 If Kim is at home, she won't be studying.   _____

6 Ling will be at work or at school in the afternoons.   _____

B **Read the sentences about people at a party. Circle the correct words to complete the sentences.**

1 Don't worry about leaving Kelly alone at a party. She's chatty and outgoing. *She'll have* / *She'll* met everyone in the room in the first ten minutes.

2 People *will* / *will be* think Luis is aloof, but he's just quiet.

3 Lauren *won't* / *won't be* make small talk. She likes to make sincere connections with people, so *she'll* / *she'll be* having very intense conversations.

4 Carl can be a little self-centered, so *he'll* / *he'll be* talking about himself at any party he goes to.

5 Jonas is not very open-minded, so *he won't* / *he won't have* continue to talk to people who disagree with him.

6 Ian is narrow-minded, so *he'll be* / *he'll have* decided who he's going to talk to before the party even starts.

3 GRAMMAR AND VOCABULARY

A **Write sentences about how different people will behave at a party this Saturday. Use the cues in parentheses.**

1 A narrow-minded person (*will* + verb) will stay away from people that look different.

_____

2 An open-minded person (*will* + verb) _____

_____

3 A chatty person (*will* + *have* + past participle) _____

_____

4 A self-centered person (*will* + *be* + *ing*) _____

_____

5 A sincere person (*will* + *have* + past participle) _____

_____

6 An aloof person (*will* + *be* + *ing*) _____

_____

ACT YOUR AGE

1 VOCABULARY: Using three-word phrasal verbs

A Complete each three-word phrasal verb with a missing word from the box. One of the words is used twice.

| against | around | back | down | for | in | ~~through~~ | to | up |

1 It's difficult to **get** _____through_____ **to** her sometimes.

2 Why do you **put** _____ **with** bad employees?

3 He tends to **look** _____ **on** others because he thinks he's better than everyone.

4 Why do I always **run up** _____ the same problems?

5 You have to **stand up** _____ what you believe in.

6 Don't take him seriously. He likes to **mess** _____ **with** people.

7 It will all **come** _____ **to** our company's main goal.

8 The new employees **fit** _____ **with** our team members really well.

9 Do you have a job to **fall** _____ **on** if this new idea doesn't work out?

10 You have to **face up** _____ your problems.

B Write the correct three-word phrasal verb from exercise 1A next to each definition.

1 feel that you belong _____ fit in with _____

2 tolerate _____

3 think you are better than someone _____

4 experience difficulties _____

5 communicate successfully _____

6 joke with _____

7 be the most important part _____

8 defend _____

9 deal with _____

10 do something easy or familiar _____

2 GRAMMAR: Uses of would

A Match 1–6 with a–f.

1 He asked me if I would let him borrow twenty dollars. ___

2 I would take that job. ___

3 When we were young, we'd play in the park together. ___

4 Would you mind opening the door for me? ___

5 I think he's a great guy, but he wouldn't be right for that job. ___

6 It's not surprising that he would want to leave early. He doesn't like parties. ___

a refer to a past habit

b make a polite request

c express an opinion in a polite way

d report a statement or question

e talk about something that is expected or typical

f talk about what someone is willing or unwilling to do

Read the sentences. Then (circle) the best next sentence.

1   Lucas is always so rude to you.

   a   I wouldn't put up with it if I were you.   **b**   He asked me if I would talk to you.

2   I can't get through to Mike.

   a   Would you mind talking to him for me?   **b**   I wouldn't do that if I were you.

3   Julia can't face up to her money problems.

   a   It's natural that she would want to avoid   **b**   She asked me if I would talk about them.
   talking about them.

4   He made a lot of money as a computer programmer.

   a   He'd always talk about changing jobs.   **b**   It's understandable that he would fall back on that job.

5   You're always messing around with Pedro, and it hurts his feelings.

   a   You'd think he would be nicer to you.   **b**   Would you try to be nicer to him?

3   GRAMMAR AND VOCABULARY

A   **Rewrite each underlined sentence. Use *would* and the cue in parentheses. Make any other necessary changes to the sentence.**

1   When I was young, I didn't fit in with other kids. <u>I liked to play by myself.</u>

   (talk about a past habit) I would play by myself.

2   He likes to mess around with people all the time. <u>I don't think he's a good candidate for a teaching job.</u>

   (express an opinion in a polite way) _____

3   I lost Kim's house keys, and I can't face up to her. <u>Do you think you could tell her for me?</u>

   (make a polite request) _____

4   She has to work late tonight. <u>She wants me to look in on her mother for her.</u>

   (report a statement or question) _____

5   You're good at standing up to bullies. <u>I'm not surprised that he called you about his problem with the kids at school.</u>

   (talk about something expected or typical) _____

6   Their neighbors are so loud. <u>I don't think I could put up with it.</u>

   (talk about what someone is willing or unwilling to do) _____

2.3 SAME HERE!

1 LISTENING

A 🔊 **2.01** **Listen and circle the correct answers.**

1 Sam wants Cathy to _____ .
   a go to the beach with him
   b get a job at his office
   c join a soccer team

2 When Cathy was young, people _____ .
   a thought she was good at sports
   b didn't think she was good at sports
   c didn't think she was good at school

3 When Sam was young, people _____ .
   a thought he disliked sports
   b didn't think he was good at sports
   c didn't think he was good at school

4 Sam and Cathy _____ .
   a had the exact same experience when they were young
   b had different experiences that made them feel the same
   c had different experiences and don't understand each other

B 🔊 **2.01** **LISTEN FOR AGREEMENT** **Listen again. Then read the sentences and write *T* (true) or *F* (false).**

1 Sam wants Cathy to join a team at work. T
2 Sam has never seen Cathy play soccer. ____
3 Cathy looks like a typical athlete. ____
4 Sam looks like a typical athlete. ____
5 Teachers accused Sam of cheating in school. ____
6 Sam went to the beach last weekend. ____
7 Sam and Cathy are going to go to the beach together this weekend. ____

2 CRITICAL THINKING

A **THINK CRITICALLY** **Do you think people judge others based on the way they look? Have you ever judged people based on how they look? Explain.**

_____

_____

_____

_____

_____

A **Complete the conversation with the missing words.**

coincidence	experience	hear	here	just	mean	relate

Max	Are you going to Hassan's annual picnic on Saturday, Jan?
Jan	No, I don't think so. Are you?
Max	No, I don't like big group events. They make me so tired.
Jan	Same ¹_____! If I went to the picnic, I'd have to rest all day Sunday.
Max	I know exactly what you ²_____ . I went to the picnic last year. It was a lot of fun, but I had to stay home and watch movies by myself the whole next day.
Jan	That's ³_____ like the time I went to my college reunion. I spent the next day watching movies and reading. I just like spending time alone, I guess.
Max	I ⁴_____ you. I love spending time alone. I did a personality quiz once, and I found out I'm an introvert.
Jan	What a ⁵_____! I'm an introvert, too. And introverts aren't shy or aloof like people think.
Max	That's right. We just need more alone time than other people do.
Jan	Yeah, I need a lot of alone time. My husband, Peter, doesn't though. He's an extrovert. He loves being around other people.
Max	I can ⁶_____ to that. My best friend Rick always wants to go to parties. He finally stopped asking me to go with him. Has that been your ⁷_____ with your husband?
Jan	Yes, exactly. He used to try to get me to go to parties with him all the time, but he finally gave up.

B **Imagine that Max's best friend, Rick, and Jan's husband, Peter, are talking. They want to go to Hassan's picnic. Write their conversation. Use at least two phrases to discuss similar experiences.**

Rick	Max doesn't want to go to Hassan's picnic on Saturday, but I do. It was really fun last year.
Peter	_____
	_____
Rick	_____
	_____
Peter	_____

READ THE LABEL

1 READING

A   **PREDICT CONTEXT** Look at the picture. What is the person doing? Read the headline of the article. What do you think the article will be about?

1   The person is

   _____ .

2   I think the article will be about

   _____ .

A LOT OF WORK FOR NOTHING?

A lot of work goes into creating a nutrition label. Calorie, fat, sugar, and nutrient content must be carefully measured for accuracy so that consumers can make informed decisions about what they eat and feed their families. However, consumers can only benefit from that information if they actually read the labels. Recently, two groups of researchers were curious about whether or not people do read nutrition labels.

One of the studies, which was conducted by the United States Food and Drug Administration, found that 50% of US adults say that they read nutrition labels all or most of the time. That means that 50% report not reading them most of the time. The study reveals that twelve percent of adults say they rarely read the labels, and surprisingly, 10% claim never to read them.

A study led by researchers at the University of Minnesota focused on which label components participants looked at. Thirty-three percent of participants said that they usually read the calorie content. Between 24% and 31% said that they read the fat, sugar, and serving size information on nutrition labels. But were the participants reporting their behavior accurately? The researchers used eye trackers to see which parts of the labels participants were actually reading. The eye-tracker data indicated that only 9% of participants read the calorie count, and a mere 1% looked at calorie, fat, sugar, and serving size information.

Why don't people actually read nutrition labels? One reason may be that they are printed in small type that may be hard to read. Another reason may be that there is too much information on them to understand them easily. Whatever the reason, the data would suggest that nutrition labels are not as effective and useful as we might have hoped they would be.

B   **IDENTIFY PURPOSE** Answer the questions.

1   What do you think is the writer's main intention in this article?

   a to entertain   **b** to inform   **c** to share personal information

2   Who do you think is the target audience for the article?

   a the general public   **b** researchers   **c** the Food and Drug Administration

2 CRITICAL THINKING

A   **THINK CRITICALLY** Why do you think people's reported behavior did not match their actual behavior?

_____

_____

_____

3 WRITING

A   Look at the bar graph. Complete each sentence. Use the words in the box and the correct percentage.

indicates	observed	~~reveals that~~	shows that

1   The graph _____ reveals that 18% _____
    don't think food labels are important.

2   As can be _____
    buy what their family likes.

3   The graph _____
    are happy with their health and diet.

4   The data _____
    get product information from other sources.

B   Write a paragraph about the graph in exercise A.
    Use expressions for referring to data.

    Why do some people never read labels?

WHY PEOPLE DON'T READ NUTRITION LABELS
(Participants were allowed to choose more than one answer.)

LABELS NOT IMPORTANT

BUY WHAT FAMILY LIKES

HAPPY WITH HEALTH AND DIET

GET NUTRITION INFORMATION SOMEWHERE ELSE

0   10   20   30   40   50   60   70   80

CHECK AND REVIEW

Read the statements. Can you do these things?

UNIT 2

Mark the boxes. ✔ I can do it. [?] I am not sure.	I can …	If you are not sure, go back to these pages in the Student's Book.
VOCABULARY	☐ use personality adjectives.	page 12
	☐ use three-word phrasal verbs.	page 14
GRAMMAR	☐ use *will* in different situations.	page 13
	☐ use *would* in different situations.	page 15
LISTENING AND SPEAKING SKILLS	☐ listen for detail in a conversation.	page 17
	☐ use expressions to discuss and compare similar experiences.	page 17
READING AND WRITING SKILLS	☐ read a report based on data.	page 18
	☐ write a paragraph about a graph.	page 19

UNIT 3 IN HINDSIGHT

3.1 I TOLD YOU SO!

1 VOCABULARY: Thought processes

A Circle the answer that completes each sentence. There may be more than one acceptable answer.

1 Let's _____ all of our options before we make our decision.

   a reject   **b** reconsider   **c** review

2 I didn't like his idea at all, so I _____ it and tried to think of a better idea.

   a rejected   **b** dismissed   **c** disregarded

3 Do you _____ any problems with our plan?

   a presume   **b** foresee   **c** envision

4 We can't _____ that everything will work out the way we hope. There might be problems that we didn't think about.

   a presume   **b** interpret   **c** dismiss

5 I'm not sure why our plan didn't work. I think we should _____ the situation and figure out what we did wrong. _____

   a presume   **b** analyze   **c** evaluate

6 How do you _____ the situation? Where do you think we made mistakes?

   a foresee   **b** envision   **c** interpret

7 It's good to look at a situation and try to figure out where it went wrong, but you shouldn't _____ on it.

   a interpret   **b** fixate   **c** reconsider

B **Complete each sentence with words from the box.**

> analyze   dismiss   disregard   envision   evaluate   foresee

1 If you want to understand a future situation, you try to _____, or _____, what will happen.

2 If you think someone is wrong about a future situation, you might _____, or _____, what they say.

3 If you want to look carefully at what happened in a past situation, you would _____, or _____, the event.

2 GRAMMAR: Variations on past unreal conditionals

A **Match the sentence halves.**

1 You'd have finished it by now …   _d_
2 If you'd asked me earlier, …   _____
3 We'd have arrived on time …   _____
4 I'd have invited you …   _____
5 If you hadn't driven so fast, …   _____
6 If I'd been there, …   _____

a if I'd known you were in town.
b I'd have been able to go with you.
c I would've said something.
d if you'd been working on it all week.
e if you hadn't taken that phone call.
f you wouldn't have been in an accident.

B **Complete the sentences with the correct forms of the verbs in parentheses.**

1 If he ___had said___ (say) that to me, I ___would've been___ (be) really angry.

2 I _____ (got) you a sandwich, if I _____ (know) you were home.

3 If I _____ (not / see) it with my own eyes, I _____ (think) he had made it all up.

4 You _____ (not / got) sick if you _____ (not / sit) next to the woman who was coughing and sneezing.

5 If you _____ (come) to the lake with us, you _____ (have) a great time.

6 We _____ (walk) here if it _____ (not / rain) so hard.

3 GRAMMAR AND VOCABULARY

A **Write sentences about the situations below. Use the verb in parentheses, a past unreal conditional, and your own ideas.**

1 The project didn't go as planned. (analyze)

 If I had analyzed the schedule, the project would have gone better _____.

2 I didn't listen to my friend's advice. (disregard)

 If I hadn't _____.

3 Henry didn't think about what went wrong with his last job. (evaluate)

 If Henry had _____.

4 You thought about potential problems. (foresee)

 You'd have _____.

5 Sonia believed the weather warnings and packed an umbrella. (dismiss)

 If she'd _____.

1 VOCABULARY: Describing emotional reactions

A **Cross out the word that doesn't belong.**

1 composed	flustered	mellow	**4** successful	victorious	defeated
2 melodramatic	hysterical	victorious	**5** helpless	resourceful	inventive
3 defensive	harmless	innocent	**6** spiteful	gracious	forgiving

B **Write the correct words from exercise 1A next to the definitions. You won't use all of the words.**

1 not hurting anyone _____

2 kind and understanding when other people make mistakes _____ , _____

3 showing extreme emotion _____ , _____

4 able to solve problems creatively _____

5 not getting excited or upset in a difficult situation _____ , _____

6 wanting to upset or hurt someone _____

7 nervous or upset _____

C **Complete the sentences with words from exercise 1B.**

1 I was so _____ after the car accident that I couldn't remember my telephone number!

2 John is always so _____ . He never gets upset, even when something goes really wrong.

3 Don't be so _____ . I'm sure you're not going to lose your job just because you spilled coffee on your boss.

4 Wow, I can't believe you were able to find a new location for the company retreat in just two days. You're so _____ !

5 I heard that you got the promotion that Mark wanted. Be careful. He can be _____ when he feels that he's been treated unfairly.

2 GRAMMAR: Commenting on the past

A **Find the errors and rewrite the sentences.**

1 You should have saw the movie with us.

_____

_____

2 They may not heard you.

_____

3 I might been studying all night.

_____

4 He could have get angry.

_____

5 It shouldn't have been ate.

_____

B (Circle) **the correct answers to complete the sentences.**

1 The soccer game was great. You *should have been / might have been* there.

2 William didn't come to Andy's birthday party. He *should not have gotten / may not have gotten* the invitation.

3 Wow, this TV is a lot cheaper here than it was online. We *couldn't have bought / shouldn't have bought* it at that store.

4 I tried to call Annie a few times last weekend to see if she wanted to hang out, but she didn't answer her phone. She *may have been working / should have been working* all weekend.

5 I heard you almost got a job at my company last year. We *should have been working / could have been working* together all this time!

3 GRAMMAR AND VOCABULARY

A **Complete the conversation. Use expressions of exaggeration or understatement and *have* + your own ideas.**

Kim I was driving to a job interview this morning, and right before I got there, the guy in front of me was driving so slowly in the parking lot.

Marco He could ¹ _____ .

Kim Yeah, he was looking for a parking spot, but I yelled at him. I was almost late and I was already stressed about the interview, so I got a little ² _____
and told him that it would be his fault if I didn't get the job. Then, when I got to the interview, the interviewer was the guy in the car!

Marco Oh, no! He might not ³ _____ .

Kim He did recognize me. He was very ⁴ _____
and laughed about it, but I was so embarrassed.

Marco How did the interview go?

Kim It was horrible. I was really ⁵ _____
so I kept dropping things and forgetting what I wanted to say. I know I didn't get the job.

Marco You shouldn't ⁶ _____ .

Kim I know. I should have been more patient. Believe me, I'm never going to yell at another driver again.

3.3 A COMPLETE DISASTER!

1 LISTENING

A 🔊 **3.01** **LISTEN FOR ATTITUDE** Listen to the conversation between Serena and her friend Zach. Then answer the questions.

1 Who did Serena have a meeting with?

2 How did her meeting go?

3 How does Serena feel about the situation?

4 How does Zach react to the story?

B 🔊 **3.01** **LISTEN FOR DETAILS** Listen to the conversation again. Check (✓) the things that happened. Write (✗) next to the things that didn't happen.

Serena showed her boss summaries of her projects for the year. ☐

Serena said something bad about a co-worker. ☐

Serena was late for her meeting with her boss. ☐

Serena asked for a raise and a promotion. ☐

Serena was in another meeting. ☐

The boss said Serena could have the raise, but not the promotion. ☐

Serena realized that she forgot to bring something to the meeting. ☐

Serena asked her boss for a new project idea. ☐

2 CRITICAL THINKING

A 🔊 **3.02** **THINK CRITICALLY** Listen to a conversation between Serena and her mother. Then answer the questions.

1 What are three ways Serena's conversation with her mother is different from her conversation with Zach?

2 What are two possible reasons that Serena's conversation with her mother is different from her conversation with Zach?

A   **Look at the clues and complete the crossword.**

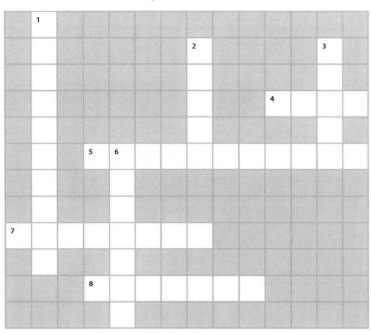

ACROSS

4   It was the worst presentation ____ !

5   It was a(n) ____ disaster.

7   Everything that could ____ go wrong did go wrong.

8   I just couldn't ____ this was happening!

DOWN

1   I think you're blowing it out of ____ .

2   You haven't heard the ____ part yet.

3   We've all been ____ .

6   I'll bet no one even ____ .

B   **Write a short conversation for each situation below. Use some of the phrases from exercise 3A.**

1   You tried out for the baseball team this morning. You haven't played in a while, so you couldn't hit the ball and you missed almost every catch. You tell your friend about it.

   You _____

   Your friend _____

   You _____

   Your friend _____

2   Your neighbor is upset because he cooked dinner for his boss last night and it was bad. He burned the chicken, the soup was too salty, and he spilled soda on his boss's expensive jacket.

   Your neighbor _____

   You _____

   Your neighbor _____

   You _____

   Your neighbor _____

1   READING

A   **CREATE COHESION**   Read the headline of the first story. What do you think it's about? Complete the statement. Then read the story to check your answer.

I think it's about _____ .

ABRAHAM LINCOLN AND JOHN F. KENNEDY: Parallel Lives?

Abraham Lincoln and John F. Kennedy were both American presidents. But the similarities between them don't stop there. Read on and find out about the remarkable coincidences in the lives and deaths of the two men.

- Lincoln became president in 1860. Kennedy had that same honor in 1960.
- The names Lincoln and Kennedy both contain seven letters.
- Both presidents were assassinated on a Friday.
- Lincoln's secretary, Kennedy, warned him not to go to the theater, where he was assassinated. Kennedy's secretary, Lincoln, warned him not to go to Dallas, where he would later be killed.
- Both their assassins were known by three names: John Wilkes Booth and Lee Harvey Oswald.
- Both men were succeeded as president by men named Johnson—Andrew and Lyndon B.

THE LINCOLN AND KENNEDY COINCIDENCES: Are they as amazing as they seem?

The long list of coincidences between Abraham Lincoln and John F. Kennedy has been circulating on the Internet for several years now. How accurate is this list? Let's examine the facts:

- The two men were elected president 100 years apart, which is no more than a satisfying round number. US Presidential elections occur every four years, or 25 times per century.
- The average length of US Presidents' names is 6.6 letters, so 7 letters is not uncommon. Also, their first names do not contain the same number of letters.
- Because there are only seven days in a week, there is a one in seven chance that they would have been assassinated on the same day of the week. In addition, the actual dates of their assassinations are different. Lincoln died on April 15, 1865 while Kennedy died on November 22, 1963.
- There is no record of Abraham Lincoln having had a secretary named Kennedy. John F. Kennedy did, indeed, have a secretary named Evelyn Lincoln, but there is no proof that she warned him not to go to Dallas. In addition, both men may have been warned on the days they were killed, but both had been warned several other times not to attend events because of threats to their lives.
- Before Kennedy's assassination, Lee Harvey Oswald went by the name Lee, not Lee Harvey. His middle name was used publicly only after the assassination. In addition, many Americans have three names—a first, a middle, and a last name.
- It's true that after both men's deaths, men named Johnson became president. However, Johnson is one of the most popular surnames in the United States. It is currently the second most common surname in the country.

B   **EVALUATE CONTENT**   Read the story and the report from a fact-checking site. Then complete the chart.

Which coincidences in the story are true?	Which are untrue?

2 CRITICAL THINKING

A **THINK CRITICALLY** Which facts make the coincidences in the story seem less significant? List two of these facts below and explain how each one lessens the impact of the story's coincidences.

1 Fact: _____

Explanation: _____

2 Fact: _____

Explanation: _____

3 WRITING

A Complete the sentences with words from the box. Not all words are used.

both	each	neither	same	together	two

1 Their last names have the _____ number of letters. _____ has seven letters.

2 _____ men were assassinated on a Friday.

3 _____ man ever served as vice-president.

4 The _____ presidents were succeeded by men named Johnson.

B Write a new version of the story about Lincoln and Kennedy's coincidences. Include only facts and use the words in exercise 3A to point out coincidences.

_____

_____

_____

_____

_____

CHECK AND REVIEW

Read the statements. Can you do these things?

UNIT 3	Mark the boxes. ☑ I can do it. ? I am not sure.	If you are not sure, go back to these pages in the Student's Book.
	I can ...	
VOCABULARY	☐ use words that describe thought processes.	page 22
	☐ describe emotional reactions.	page 24
GRAMMAR	☐ use past unreal conditionals.	page 23
	☐ comment on the past.	page 25
LISTENING AND SPEAKING SKILLS	☐ listen for attitude in a conversation.	page 26
	☐ offer sympathy and reassurance.	page 27
READING AND WRITING SKILLS	☐ read two stories and evaluate their content.	page 29
	☐ write a short paragraph based on facts.	page 29

4.1 · UNDER THE MICROSCOPE

1 VOCABULARY: Describing things

A Write a word from the box that has the same or the opposite meaning. You will not use one of the words.

circular	cylindrical	delicate	elaborate	filthy	flaky
miniature	multicolored	ridged	~~spiral~~	stringy	

The same meaning

1 twisting _____spiral_____

2 round _____

3 tube-shaped _____

4 crumbly _____

5 colorful _____

The opposite meaning

6 mammoth _____

7 clean _____

8 strong _____

9 smooth _____

10 simple _____

B Complete the sentences with words from exercise 1A.

1 Microphotography can make tiny things look _____.

2 The _____ wings of a butterfly, which normally don't look very strong, can look like iron gates in a microphotograph.

3 A microphotograph might reveal that something that normally looks tan or brown, such as sand, is actually _____.

4 Something that looks basic, like a fly's eye, might really be very _____ and complex.

5 Something that appears to be dirt-free might, in fact, look _____ close up.

2 GRAMMAR: Quantifiers and prepositions in relative clauses

A (Circle) the correct phrase to complete the sentences.

1 Insect bodies, *most of which / each of which / many of whom* look smooth to the naked eye, can look rough up close.

2 Microphotography can surprise people, *most of which / many of whom / each of whom* have never wondered what insects look like up close.

3 Insects, *each of which / most of whom / many of which* have intricately formed wings and eyes, are more complex than they seem.

4 Microphotographs of bees, for instance, allow us to see their eyes, *most of which / many of which / each of which* is covered in tiny hairs.

5 Microphotographs of insects were shown to some people, *each of which / most of whom / most of which* could not guess what the photos depicted.

26

B **Correct the mistakes in the sentences.**

1 My friends, most of ~~which~~ *whom* go to my school, are coming to my birthday party.

2 I don't know what happened in the movie, which I wasn't really paying attention.

3 We enjoyed all of the dishes, each of them had been prepared by a different person.

4 I finally finished the homework, which I just found out about it.

5 My closet is full of clothes, which most of them I never wear.

C **Read the art review. Complete the online article with *each/many/most/all/none/*or *some* + *of* and *which* or *whom*. Different answers may be possible.**

●●● < >   🔍 🏠

Tonight, I'm at a photography exhibition titled "Up Close and Personal." It's an exhibition of microphotography. A lot of the exhibitors come from the world of science. Microphotographers, [1] _____ are scientists, but [2] _____ are not, are interested in seeing what things look like close up.

The microphotos, [3] _____ show us an object or a living thing from a different perspective, are fascinating to look at. A photo of sand, for example, shows us individual grains, [4] _____ has its own unique shape.

Exhibition-goers can't buy the photos, [5] _____ are for sale. After the exhibition in the gallery, the photos are going to be donated to museums, [6] _____ are science-based. These museums want to get their visitors interested in science.

3 GRAMMAR AND VOCABULARY

A **Read some more sentences from the art review and complete the sentences with your own ideas. Use the phrases in parentheses.**

1 (are elaborate and) The photos, each of which offers us a close-up view of a different subject,
   are elaborate and show us the world from a different perspective .

2 (all of which) From the position of a photography fan, I couldn't choose a favorite from among the photos,
   _____ .

3 (all of whom) We had a chance to learn about the photos from the standpoint of the photographers,
   _____ .

4 (mammoth) The photos of plants and flowers, all of which were beautiful,
   _____ .

5 (miniature) Microphotographers, many of whom are scientists,
   _____ .

27

4.2 EYE TO EYE

1 VOCABULARY: Eye idioms and metaphors

A Match each idiom or metaphor with its meaning.

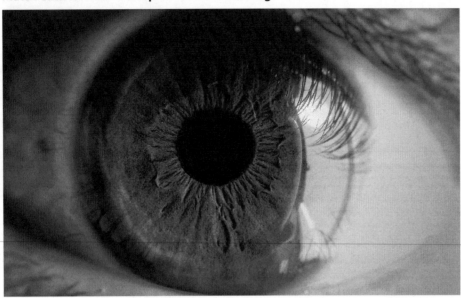

1	a bird's eye view of something	_____
2	feast your eyes on something	_____
3	see eye to eye on something	_____
4	keep your eyes on the prize	_____
5	turn a blind eye to something	_____
6	catch somebody's eye	_____
7	in the public eye	_____
8	in your mind's eye	_____
9	without batting an eye	_____
10	have eyes in the back of your head	_____
11	in the blink of an eye	_____

a to remember to think about the end goal

b to attract someone

c a view from above

d to ignore an illegal or harmful activity

e to look at something with great pleasure

f to agree with someone

g famous and in view of the whole world

h without hesitation

i to be aware of everything that is happening

j in your imagination

k instantly

B Complete each sentence with the correct form of an idiom or metaphor from exercise 1A.

1 I think my mother <u>has eyes in the back of her head</u> . I can never hide anything from her.

2 She must have a lot of money. She paid $5,000 for that ring _____ .

3 Jackie and I don't _____ . We disagree all the time.

4 That photo really _____ . I think it's beautiful.

5 He was gone _____ . I turned away for one second, and when I turned back around he had disappeared.

6 I would hate to live my life _____ . I don't know how celebrities deal with it.

7 I can't remember the address of the gallery, but I can see it _____ . It's a black building with a red door.

8 It seems the police have decided to _____ the fact that people always speed on this road. I guess they don't think it's a big deal.

2 GRAMMAR: Noun clauses with question words

A   **For each noun or noun phrase, write a question word that you can use as a substitute.**

1 the people _____ 3 reasons _____ 5 the place _____

2 things _____ 4 the way _____

B   **Rewrite each sentence with the question word in parentheses.**

1 I'm amazed by all of the things that the human eye can do.

   (what) I'm amazed by what the human eye can do _____.

2 It's interesting to see the ways that different animals' eyes developed.

   (how) _____.

3 There are so many interesting facts to share about eyes that I'm not sure which fact to begin with.

   (what) _____.

4 Because eyes are so unique, we can use them to prove that we are the people that we say we are.

   (who) _____.

5 No one really knows the reasons that the human eye developed the way it did.

   (why) _____.

6 The photographers explained the way they took their photos.

   (how) _____.

3 GRAMMAR AND VOCABULARY

A   **Complete the sentences to write an advertisement for a museum exhibit about eyes.**

Come to **THE MICROPHOTOGRAPHY EXHIBIT** *at the Science Museum!*

Feast your eyes on [1] _____.
Find out why [2] _____.
Learn how [3] _____.
See what [4] _____.
Get a bird's eye view of [5] _____.

Beautiful photos of eyes!

Why can't we see colors in the dark?

How do eagles and tigers see?

What do sharks and eagles see?

What does the world look like from an eagle's perspective?

LOOK AWAY!

1 LISTENING

A 🔊 **4.01** **LISTEN FOR MAIN IDEA** Listen to the first half of the podcast. Then write answers to the questions.

1 What does Samantha want to know?

2 What harmful activity does Dr. Chang talk about?

B 🔊 **4.01** **LISTEN FOR DETAILS** Listen again and read the statements. Write *T* for true or *F* for false.

1 You'll damage your eyes anytime you go outside without eye protection. ____

2 Going out regularly without sun protection can lead to eye diseases, cancer, and vision damage. ____

3 Summer is the most important time of year to wear sunglasses. ____

4 In the winter, the risk of sun damage to your eyes is higher if there's snow outside. ____

5 You need sunglasses with UV protection to protect your eyes. ____

C 🔊 **4.02** **LISTEN FOR DETAILS** Listen to the second half of the podcast. Then check (✓) all the correct answers.

> **According to Dr. Chang, rubbing your eyes is a bad habit because**
> ☐ you can scratch your eyes.
> ☐ you can get allergies.
> ☐ you have germs on your hands.
> ☐ you can get an eye infection.
> ☐ you can damage your corneas.
> ☐ you can develop certain eye conditions, such as myopia or glaucoma.
> ☐ you can break blood vessels around your eyes.

2

SPEAKING

A   Complete the sentences with expressions
    from the box. Not all expressions will be used.

comes down to
getting at the heart of
in itself
key to
major impact
objectively
straightforward
there's considerably more to it
truth of the matter is

Samantha   Can we talk about diet and how it affects eye health?

Dr. Chang   Ah, now we're [1] _____ how our daily habits affect our eyes. Your diet can have a [2] _____ on your eye health. The [3] _____ having healthy eyes is eating foods rich in certain nutrients, such as Vitamin C, lutein, zinc, and omega-3 fatty acids.

Samantha   I see. Is there anything else we should be aware of?

Dr. Chang   Well, the issue is pretty [4] _____ . If you're not getting the vitamins and minerals that you need, it's not likely that your eyes will be healthy.

Samantha   Are there any common household items that can harm our eyes?

Dr. Chang   The [5] _____ there are a lot of chemicals in the average home that can cause severe eye damage. Household cleaners, for instance, can cause a variety of problems from mild irritation to loss of vision.

Samantha   How can we avoid injuring our eyes when we're cleaning?

Dr. Chang   It really [6] _____ protecting your eyes any time you work with dangerous chemicals.

B   **Think of three things you've learned in this unit about keeping your eyes healthy. Then write a conversation, giving someone advice about how to keep his/her eyes healthy. Use at least three expressions from exercise 2A.**

A   What are some tips for keeping my eyes healthy? _____

B   _____

A   _____

B   _____

A   _____

B   _____

A   _____

B   _____

1 READING

A **READ FOR MAIN IDEA** **Read the blog post. Which sentence best summarizes the whole post? <u>Underline</u> it.**

Seeing Things from a Different Perspective

Do you tend to get stuck in details and forget about the big picture? Being detail-oriented can help you get things done, but if you focus exclusively on details, you might never accomplish, or even think about, your bigger life goals. The good news is that your attention to detail can actually help you reach your life goals once you've defined them.

The first step in improving your ability to see the big picture is to actually devote time to the task. It can be easy to become so focused on details that you go from one small task to another without taking a break. Take some time out of each day to stop and think about your big goals. For example, is there a career that you want to have in the future? Do you want to

get a degree? Do you want to write a book, live in a different city, become fluent in a new language? Envision yourself having achieved that goal.

Now, this is where your attention to detail comes into play. With your eventual outcome clear in your mind's eye, list the steps that you have to take to meet your goal. Writing details on sticky notes, sticking them on a wall, and looking at them all together might help you get a bird's eye view of the situation.

Finally, write your big goal down and post it somewhere where you can see it every day. The daily reminder will help you remember to keep your eyes on the prize and not get so buried in details that you lose sight of your ultimate goal.

B **READ FOR DETAILS** **Complete the summary of the blog post with phrases from the box. Not all phrases will be used.**

see the big picture	thinking about
achieving those goals	talking about
focus on details	time for reaching
steps toward achieving	writing it down

You can use your ability to [1] _____
to achieve big-picture life goals. First, spend time
[2] _____ your life goals and see
yourself [3] _____ . Next, consider
the necessary [4] _____ your big
goals. Finally, remind yourself of that big-picture goal every
day by [5] _____ and putting it
somewhere you can see it.

2 CRITICAL THINKING

A **THINK CRITICALLY** **Write an answer to the question.**

What other kinds of goals do you think the tips in the blog post could help you achieve? Explain.

_____

_____

_____

A **Put the words in the correct order to complete the phrases.**

1 track / record / successful

with a _____

2 problems / practical / to / solving / approach

with a _____

3 marketing / double / major / and business / in

as a _____

4 world / startups / to dot-com

from the corporate

_____

5 for / eye / keen / detail

with a _____

B **Choose one of the jobs from the box and list the skills and qualities that you think it requires. Then write a personal statement for an ideal candidate for the job you chose. Make your statement clear and concise.**

office manager for a busy lawyer's office	volunteer coordinator for a high school
computer programmer for an app developer	visiting nurse (visiting patients at home)

Skills and Qualities:

_____

_____

Ideal Candidate:

_____

_____

CHECK AND REVIEW

Read the statements. Can you do these things?

UNIT 4	Mark the boxes. ☑ I can do it. ? I am not sure.		If you are not sure, go back to these pages in the Student's Book.
	I can ...		
VOCABULARY	☐ describe things.	page 34	
	☐ use eye idioms and metaphors.	page 36	
GRAMMAR	☐ use quantifiers and prepositions in relative clauses.	page 35	
	☐ use noun clauses with question words.	page 37	
LISTENING AND SPEAKING SKILLS	☐ listen for details in a podcast.	page 38	
	☐ clarify a problem and give advice.	page 39	
READING AND WRITING SKILLS	☐ read for gist and detail in a blog post.	page 40	
	☐ write a personal statement for a job candidate.	page 41	

UNIT 5 REMOTE

5.1 THE END OF THE ROAD

1 VOCABULARY: Describing remote places

A **Cross out the word that is different in meaning.**

1	~~crowded~~	barren	deserted		5	scenic	ugly	beautiful
2	unspoiled	untouched	ruined		6	bare	lush	abundant
3	immense	isolated	vast		7	harsh	friendly	hostile
4	well-known	anonymous	nameless					

B **Circle the best word to complete each sentence.**

1 It's easy to get lost in the forest if you don't know where you're going because it's … .

    a immense   **b** nameless   **c** unspoiled

2 A lot of people go to the mountains to enjoy the … landscape.

    a barren   **b** hostile   **c** scenic

3 The desert can be a very … place. It is often extremely hot in the daylight hours and freezing cold at night.

    a picturesque   **b** hostile   **c** abundant

4 It's difficult to find a place that is … . Most places have been visited by people.

    a vast   **b** unspoiled   **c** abandoned

5 The area around the lake was … with trees, plants, and flowers.

    a barren   **b** deserted   **c** lush

2 GRAMMAR: Participle phrases in initial position

A **Check (✓) the correct sentences. Then correct the mistakes in the incorrect sentences.**

1 Having ~~to lose~~ ^{lost} our map, we couldn't find our way out of the forest. ☐

2 Exhausting from climbing, we finally reached the top of the hill. ☐

3 Sitting at the top of the hill, we could see a vast scenic landscape in front of us. ☐

4 Amazed at the beauty of our surroundings, we were speechless. ☐

5 Having to find a quiet peaceful spot to rest, we put down our packs and had lunch. ☐

6 Looking for unspoiled locations they traveled all over the country. ☐

34

B **Put the words in the correct order to make sentences. Start each sentence with a participle phrase. Add commas in the correct places.**

1 spot to / a remote / camp / we found / wandering / through the woods
   <u>Wandering through the woods, we found a remote spot to camp.</u>

2 the spot we found / our tents / we started / excited / putting up / by

3 wood for / having set / began / to gather / up our tents / a fire / we

4 of / our dinner / the fire / seated / in front / we cooked

5 scary stories / and told / having / we / relaxed / eaten dinner

6 we went / of hiking / long day / to sleep / tired / from a / early

7 our tents / we heard / animals / lying in / of forest / the sounds

3 GRAMMAR AND VOCABULARY

A **Write sentences about the two photos below using the prompts. Start each sentence with a participle phrase.**

1 walk through the immense area / you
   <u>Walking through the immense area, you might get lost.</u>

2 unspoiled by humans / the forest

3 find this scenic place / you

4 deserted decades ago / the town

5 look at the town now / it's hard to believe / it

6 abandon their homes / residents

HOW TO BE ALONE

1 VOCABULARY: Talking about influences

A **Write *N* for noun, *V* for verb, or *B* for words that can be either nouns or verbs.**

1 consequence N
2 stem from ___
3 influence ___
4 motivate ___
5 impact ___
6 trigger ___
7 result in ___
8 force ___
9 source ___
10 result in ___
11 implications ___

B (Circle) **the correct words and phrases to complete the paragraph.**

I used to be a truck driver, transporting food and other goods from one city to another. The job paid well, but working as a truck driver had a negative ¹*source /* (*impact*) on my life. The problem was the fact that I was alone for days at a time. Sometimes my trips lasted over a week. ²*The source / The consequence* of this was that I had trouble making and keeping friends. This ³*stemmed from / resulted in* not being home long enough to spend time with other people. When I did have a couple of days to spend at home, I was so tired from driving that I just wanted to sleep and relax. On my birthday last year, I realized that I didn't have anyone to spend my day with. That experience finally ⁴*motivated / impacted* me to change jobs. Now I deliver mail in my own city. My job change ⁵*has impacted / has triggered* my life in positive ways. I work regular hours and get off of work at 5:00, so I have time to hang out with friends. I also have more energy than I did when I was on the road all day. Another truck driver that I know is thinking about a job change. I'm hoping that my positive experience will ⁶*influence / stem from* him and encourage him to take that step like I did.

2 GRAMMAR: Reduced relative clauses

A **Read the reduced relative clauses and add a relative pronoun and the correct form of *be* to each one.**

1 People ∧ *who are* uncomfortable being alone all day should not work as truck drivers.

2 Lighthouses, usually far from cities and towns, are lonesome places.

3 Working alone is a good solution for anyone in need of time to themselves.

4 Writers, able to make their own schedules, often find themselves working odd hours.

5 Swimming pool lifeguards, usually surrounded by other people, can't spend time talking to those people because they have to focus on watching swimmers.

B   **Combine the two sentences using a complete relative clause. Then cross out two words to form a reduced relative clause.**

1   Some people are happy being alone. These people enjoy being lighthouse keepers or truck drivers.

   Some people, ~~who are~~ happy being alone, enjoy being lighthouse keepers or truck drivers.

2   Someone might be thinking about getting a job that requires solitude. They should consider it carefully before they make a decision.

3   Solitude is a problem for some people. It isn't a problem for me.

4   Some people are lonely because they work alone. They should get together with friends at least once a month.

5   Is anyone able to go without speaking to someone for a whole week? I don't know anyone who can do that.

6   I work in a remote area. The area is fifty miles away from the nearest town.

3 GRAMMAR AND VOCABULARY

A   **Complete the sentences with words from the box and your own ideas. Use reduced relative clauses when possible.**

impact	result in	source	trigger

1   The _____root_____ of my problem is the never-ending solitude _____required by my job_____ .

2   Working alone would have a positive _____ on an individual _____ .

3   Working alone all day can _____ some people to create networks with other people _____ .

4   Working remotely can be very isolating and _____ feelings of loneliness for people _____ .

5   Solitude can _____ depression for people _____ .

5.3 WORKING FROM HOME

1 LISTENING

A 🔊 **5.01** **LISTEN FOR THE MAIN IDEA** **Listen to the discussion. Then write answers to the questions.**

1 Where are the speakers?

2 What is Leah suggesting?

B 🔊 **5.01** **LISTEN FOR DETAILS** **Listen again and circle all the correct answers.**

1 Who likes the idea of working from home?

    a Jack   **b** Fatima   **c** Jack and Martin   **d** Jack and Fatima

2 Who can't concentrate in the office?

    a Jack   **b** Leah   **c** Jack and Leah   **d** Fatima and Martin

3 Who drives at least thirty minutes to get to work?

    a Fatima   **b** Jack and Martin   **c** Fatima and Martin   **d** Leah and Fatima

C **DIFFERENTIATE FACTS AND OPINIONS** **Read the excerpts from the meeting and write _O_ (opinion) or _F_ (fact).**

1 … other departments in this company have started allowing people to work from home a few days a week. _F_

2 We thought that this might hurt productivity … _____

3 … employees in those departments have increased their productivity by 30%. _____

4 In the past twelve months, productivity in this department has steadily decreased. _____

5 … I really think that we need to make a change in our department … _____

6 Working from home sounds like a great solution to my problem. _____

7 I would be able to concentrate better at home. _____

8 Also, I live more than thirty minutes away from the office. _____

2 CRITICAL THINKING

A **THINK CRITICALLY** **Why do you think Leah thought letting people work from home would hurt productivity?**

3

SPEAKING

A   **Which phrases fit in each sentence? Write them in the correct places in the chart.**

As a result of The outcomes of	Because of Thanks to	Consequently, That's why	Due to The consequences of	For these reasons,

	… the change, productivity has increased.
	… we've decided to allow people to work from home.
	… this have been happier employees and higher productivity.

B   **Imagine that your company has decided to let you work from home three days a week. List some possible effects of this change. Then use four of your ideas to complete the sentences.**
Possible Effects:

1 Due to this change, _____ .
2 One consequence of _____ .
3 Thanks to the fact that I can work from home _____ .
4 For these reasons, _____ .

REMOTE SUCCESS STORY

1 READING

A **PREDICT CONTENT** Look at the title of the article and the visual. What do you think the article is going to be about?

_____

B **READ FOR MAIN IDEA** Read the article and (circle) the best summary of it.

a Lullabot, 100% remote from the very beginning, benefits from having a completely remote workforce.

b Lullabot, a website strategy, design and development company, has decided to allow all of its employees to begin working from home.

c Lullabot, a Rhode Island-based company, explains the advantages and disadvantages of having a remote workforce.

REMOTE FROM THE START

Lullabot, based in Providence, Rhode Island, is a website strategy, design, and development company. Unlike many companies, which move toward remote work after being fully established, Lullabot's employees have been working remotely since day one. Today, the company's employees are distributed all over the world.

As a result of having all their employees working remotely, the company has had to make communication with them a priority from the start. As Jared Ponchot, the company's creative director, points out, when a company begins to move from a traditional model to a remote model, it has to deal with certain difficulties. For example, the first employees to work remotely end up feeling out of the loop. This may be due to the fact that the company continues to operate as if all of its workers are in-house, and doesn't make the changes needed to make sure that remote workers are included in everything. Owing to the fact that they began with a fully remote team, Lullabot has necessarily become adept at keeping everyone well-informed.

Being 100% remote has had positive effects on Lullabot's employees. Although Lullabot has standard business hours, the company's employees are able to have flexible schedules as long as they're meeting their work-related obligations. In addition, they have the time and the space to do their most creative work without unnecessary interruptions. All-in-all, Lullabot sounds like a great company to work for.

C **READ FOR DETAILS** Find three examples of cause-and-effect expressions in the article. What alternatives might you use if you were telling a friend the same information?

1 Example: _____

Alternative: _____

2 Example: _____

Alternative: _____

3 Example: _____

Alternative: _____

2 CRITICAL THINKING

A **THINK CRITICALLY** What would you say the writer's attitude toward Lullabot is? Find two examples to support your opinion.

_____

_____

A **CREATE COHESION** Use participial phrases to connect the ideas and reduce the information to one sentence. Check your work by referring to the text above.

1 Lullabot began as a remote company. Lullabot's management has a lot of experience with remote workers.

  Having begun as a remote company, Lullabot's management has a lot of experience with remote workers.

2 Lullabot's employees can work wherever they want to. The employees can choose workspaces where they feel most comfortable.

_____

3 Other companies see Lullabot as a successful remote company. Lullabot is a good model for other companies that want to go remote.

_____

B Use the information in the box to write a profile of a company. Include at least two introductory participle phrases and two phrases to show cause and effect.

> MobileApp Company—App Designer and Developer
> - Everyone works remotely on Wednesday through Friday.
> - Employees are more productive at home.
> - No commuting means employees are less stressed.
> - Employees are more creative when they're not stressed.
> - The company is considering becoming 100% remote.

_____
_____
_____
_____
_____
_____
_____

CHECK AND REVIEW

Read the statements. Can you do these things?

UNIT 5	Mark the boxes. ☑ I can do it. ？ I am not sure. I can …	If you are not sure, go back to these pages in the Student's Book.
VOCABULARY	☐ describe remote places.	page 44
	☐ talk about influences.	page 46
GRAMMAR	☐ use participle phrases in initial position.	page 45
	☐ use reduced relative clauses.	page 47
LISTENING AND SPEAKING SKILLS	☐ differentiate facts and opinions in a discussion.	page 48
	☐ discuss the effects of working remotely.	page 49
READING AND WRITING SKILLS	☐ analyze the content of an article.	page 50
	☐ write a company profile.	page 51

6.1   THE SURPRISE BUSINESS

1   VOCABULARY: Using adverbs to add attitude

A   **Match the words with their meanings.**

1	truly	___	**a**	visibly
2	as expected	___	**b**	utterly
3	clearly	___ , ___	**c**	understandably
4	very	___ , ___	**d**	genuinely
			e	immensely
			f	noticeably

B   **Complete the story with the words from the box.**

anxious	calm	helpful
popular	shaken	~~shocked~~
surprised	thrilled	unusual
upset		

Marta was utterly ¹_____*shocked*_____ when her best friend, Lisa, gave her a gift certificate for a helicopter ride for her birthday. Lisa had bought the certificate from an immensely ²_____ company that was known to give helicopter rides to celebrities. It was a highly ³_____ gift, just like all of Lisa's birthday presents.

Marta looked visibly ⁴_____ by the idea of going up in a helicopter. Lisa was genuinely ⁵_____ to see Marta's reaction to her gift. What Lisa didn't know was that Marta was deeply ⁶_____ about flying. She was understandably ⁷_____ that she had given Marta a gift that she didn't want. However, she stayed remarkably ⁸_____ , even though she felt terrible.

Lisa called the helicopter company and asked if she could get a refund. The person she talked to was incredibly ⁹_____ and gave her a full refund. Lisa used the money to buy her friend a day at the spa instead. Marta was noticeably ¹⁰_____ by the new gift, and the two friends spent a nice, relaxing day at the spa with both feet firmly on the ground.

2   GRAMMAR: Clefts

A   **Check (✓) the correct sentences. Then correct the mistakes in the incorrect sentences.**

1   The thing that I most try to avoid it̶ is spiders.   ☐

2   What I didn't expect was to have lunch with my favorite actor.   ☐

3   What I hate most it is being surprised.   ☐

4   The reason why that surprises scare me.   ☐

5   It wasn't until it was all over that I was able to calm down.   ☐

6   The gifts that I enjoy most the ones that I never expected.   ☐

B   **Complete the sentences. Match 1–8 with a–h.**

1   What I didn't expect was ___f___
2   The thing I love most is _____
3   The reason why I'm late is _____
4   What I love about traveling is _____
5   It wasn't until I got home _____
6   The place I most want to visit is _____
7   What I love most about my job is _____
8   What I never expected was _____

a   taking walks on the beach.
b   Istanbul, Turkey.
c   meeting new people in new places.
d   that I would enjoy living in a big city.
e   that I realized that I had lost my scarf.
f   that we'd spend the day on a boat.
g   that my car broke down.
h   the people that I work with.

3   GRAMMAR AND VOCABULARY

A   **Complete the sentences to make them true for you.**

1   What makes me understandably upset is when someone _____
_____ .

2   The thing that makes me most deeply anxious is when I have to _____
_____ .

3   My best friend was noticeably thrilled when _____
_____ .

4   The person I find most helpful is _____
because _____ .

5   One thing that makes me remarkably calm is _____
_____ .

6   The time I was utterly shocked was _____
_____ .

7   The most immensely popular place I've ever been to is _____
_____ .

8   The last time I was genuinely surprised was _____
_____ .

1 VOCABULARY: Using the prefixes *under-* and *over-*

A **Look at the clues and complete the crossword.**

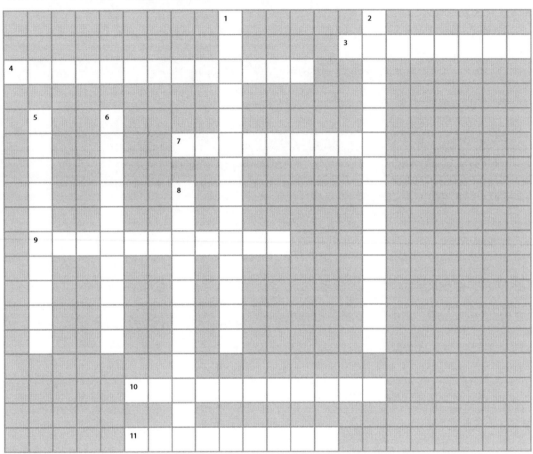

Across

3 the person or team is considered to be the weakest and the least likely to win a competition

4 feeling too sure about yourself

7 thought to be better than it is

9 feeling like you have too much to deal with

10 costing less than something is worth

11 not getting enough money for your work

Down

1 having thought that someone has less power or ability than they have

2 not advanced as much as something should be

5 made to work too much

6 costing more than something is worth

8 having too many people in one place

B **Complete each sentence with a word from exercise 1A. Change the prefix if necessary.**

1 This movie is _____. It's not as good as everyone says it is.

2 I have so much work to do. I'm feeling _____.

3 We really _____ how many people were going to be at this party. We didn't make enough food!

4 You should charge more for your paintings. I think they're _____.

5 I think I'm _____. I just found out that other people in this company are making a lot more money than I am.

2 GRAMMAR: Question words with -*ever*

A Complete the sentences. Match 1–6 with a–f.

1   You should do   *b*   a   it's far from here.

2   We can leave   ___   b   whatever you want.

3   I'll get the money for school   ___   c   make sure you tell him the news.

4   Wherever he lives,   ___   d   didn't leave a message.

5   However you contact him,   ___   e   whenever you're ready.

6   Whoever called you   ___   f   however I can.

B Complete each sentence with the correct question word from the box.

| however | whatever | whenever | wherever | whichever | whoever |

1   I see that woman _____ I go! She's everywhere!

2   I don't think you should do it. It's a bad idea _____ you look at it.

3   Look at that guy over there. _____ he is, he looks just like your brother.

4   Are you still trying to decide which school to go to? _____ school you choose, I'm
    sure you'll enjoy college.

5   I've applied to ten different jobs in the last month. _____ I do, I just can't get a job!

6   I can't ride in the back of the car. _____ I do, I get sick.

3 GRAMMAR AND VOCABULARY

A Complete the conversations with words from the box and question words with -*ever*.

| overcrowded | overpriced | overrated | ~~underestimated~~ |

1   **A** I just watched a movie called *Miracle on Ice*. I guess everyone really <u>underestimated</u> Team USA's abilities.

    B <u>However you look at it</u> , it was an amazing moment in sports history.

2   **A** I'm not sure which car to buy. This car is _____ , but it's in really good condition.
       The other car needs some work, but the price is great.

    B _____ , make sure you get
       good insurance.

3   **A** We went to the beach today, and it was really
       _____ . We couldn't
       find a place to sit.

    B _____ , there are
       always too many people there.

4   **A** Are you sure you want to go to this restaurant?
       I think it might be _____ .
       John went there last week and said it's not as
       good as we've heard.

    B I'll do _____ you want.
       We can go somewhere else if you want.

6.3 A SURPRISING COMEBACK

1 LISTENING

A 🔊 **6.01** **LISTEN FOR MAIN POINTS** **Listen to a podcast episode about the Maker Movement. Circle the two main points.**

a Lila Marcus makes jewelry and is a ceramics artist.

b Makers are people who make things, such as clothing, furniture, and jewelry, instead of buying things.

c Buying handmade goods is better for the economy than buying things from corporate-owned stores.

d Social media and websites are full of information about how to make things instead of buying them.

e An increasing number of people are learning to make things themselves.

B 🔊 **6.01** **LISTEN FOR DETAILS** **Listen again. Write *T* (true) or *F* (false). Correct the false statements.**

1 Makers ~~don't~~ use tools. __F__

2 The important thing for makers is that they make handmade goods. ___

3 The Maker Movement started a few years ago. ___

4 It was immediately obvious that the Maker Movement was starting. ___

5 Lila talks about websites that teach you how to make things yourself. ___

6 Some makers are starting their own businesses, but they're not successful. ___

7 Lila thinks that people stopped making things because they could buy better products in stores. ___

8 Lila believes that the Maker Movement is happening because makers want to learn skills that people had in the past. ___

C 🔊 **6.02** **Listen to the sentences and circle the words that you hear.**

1	really	actually	(simply)
2	actually	really	even
3	even	simply	actually
4	simply	even	really
5	didn't know	did know	do know
6	exactly right	totally obsessed	genuinely delighted

46

2 SPEAKING

A **Circle** the correct word or phrase to complete each sentence.

Matthew So, Lila, tell me about what you like to make.

Lila Well, I've been a maker for a long time. I design and sew my own clothes. I make jewelry, and I make ceramic pieces, like plates, bowls, and mugs. I ¹**even** / simply made my own kitchen table.

Matthew Wow, that must have been challenging.

Lila It ²even / **really** was.

Matthew You've been able to make a successful business out of your crafts, right?

Lila Yes, that's right. I sell my jewelry online. It wasn't ³immediately clear / exactly right to me at first which of my crafts I should sell. However, ⁴what I enjoyed making most was / what I enjoyed making most were jewelry, so I decided to go with that.

Matthew Were you successful right away?

Lila No, I wasn't. ⁵Even / Actually, for the first few months, I didn't sell anything at all. I started to worry, but then a friend of mine helped me redesign my website and I started an Instagram account for my jewelry. I didn't know if it was going to work, but then it ⁶does / did help a lot. I was ⁷extremely anxious / genuinely thrilled when that happened.

B **Read the information in the box about Eli, a maker who makes furniture. Then complete the interview between Matthew and Eli. Use at least four words or phrases for adding emphasis.**

makes tables, chairs, cabinets, sofas	is successful
sells furniture online and in stores	was successful right away
shocked when people started buying his furniture	advice: Don't give up!

Matthew Tell me about what you like to make, Eli.

Eli _____

_____

Matthew Have you been able to create a successful business?

Eli _____

_____

Matthew Was your business immediately successful?

Eli _____

_____

Matthew What are some tips you would give to a maker who wants to start a business?

Eli _____

_____

JUMP SCARE

1 READING

A **PREDICT CONTENT** Look at the headlines. Match each headline to the correct topic.

1 The Face of Fear _____
2 Fear for Fun _____
3 Overcoming Fear _____
4 Fight or Flight Response _____

a why we enjoy being scared
b how our bodies react to fear
c what we look like when we're scared
d how to deal with our fears

B **READ FOR MAIN IDEAS** Read the stories and write the correct headline for each one. Use two of the headlines from exercise 1A.

A _____

Imagine that you're sitting in your dark living room watching a scary movie. The main character hears a noise in the basement. She decides to go down to see what it is. As a viewer, you know that there's a monster in the basement and the main character shouldn't go downstairs. You also know that at some point soon, the monster is going to jump out at the main character. Still, even though you're expecting it, you jump. What does your face look like at this moment? If you were genuinely scared, your eyes would be wide and your mouth open. Why does this happen? Scientist Charles Darwin had an explanation. He found that when we are scared, we instinctively tighten our muscles, even the muscles in our face. This is so we are ready to defend ourselves or run away if we have to. When we are truly scared, we can't avoid tightening these muscles, and inevitably, we make the face of fear.

B _____

When you feel scared, whether it's for a moment when someone jumps out at you from behind a door, or for several minutes while you wonder if the noise you hear outside is a burglar or just your neighbor's cat, your body changes in certain ways. Some of these changes are noticeable. Your heart beats faster, your breathing rate increases, and your face might become flushed or get very pale. Other changes are not visible. Your blood vessels become wider, your digestion slows down or might even stop, and your hearing and vision become very focused. All of these changes are part of your fight or flight response to fear, and they help you fight off an attacker or get away as fast as you can. For example, wider blood vessels allow more blood to get to your muscles so they are stronger. Your digestion slows down because your body needs all its energy to deal with the current threat. And your hearing and vision change so you can locate a threat more easily.

2 CRITICAL THINKING

A **THINK CRITICALLY** How do you think the fight or flight response might have helped humans 15,000 years ago? How might it not be as useful to us now?

_____

_____

_____

3 WRITING

A Read this summary of one of the topics below based on information from the two texts in exercise 1B. Which topic is it summarizing? Circle the topic.

why we like to be scared   why fear makes us react in certain ways

All of the changes that happen in our bodies when we're afraid help us to deal with the threat we are facing. Our physical reactions help us become stronger so we can locate a threat, fight against it, or run away from it.

B Write a short summary of the topic that wasn't summarized in exercise 3A.

_____

_____

_____

_____

_____

_____

_____

_____

CHECK AND REVIEW

Read the statements. Can you do these things?

UNIT 6	Mark the boxes. ☑ I can do it. ? I am not sure.	If you are not sure, go back to these pages in the Student's Book.
	I can ...	
VOCABULARY	☐ use adverbs to add attitude.	page 54
	☐ use the prefixes *under-* and *over-*.	page 56
GRAMMAR	☐ use clefts.	page 55
	☐ use question words with *-ever*.	page 57
LISTENING AND SPEAKING SKILLS	☐ listen for details in a podcast.	page 58
	☐ use phrases to add emphasis.	page 59
READING AND WRITING SKILLS	☐ read two stories and identify the main focus.	page 60
	☐ write a short summary of a topic.	page 61

1.5 TIME TO SPEAK Professor Robot?

A   Think of three tasks that you don't like to do and wish a robot could do for you. Complete the chart.

What is the task?	Why don't you like to do it?	How do you think a robot could do it better?

B   Create an advertisement for your robot. In the advertisement, describe what tasks the robot could do and why it could do it better than a human could. Share your ad in the next class.

2.5 TIME TO SPEAK Labeled out

A   Create a survey about brand-name foods (well-known brands) vs. generic brands (usually less expensive versions of well-known brands). Write four questions to ask.

B   Survey your friends and family.

C   Bring your survey results to your next class and present your results.

3.5 TIME TO SPEAK The ripple effect

A   Make a list of effects that you have had on your environment and the people in your life.

_____

_____

_____

_____

_____

B   Choose the three most significant effects and imagine how the world would be different if you hadn't been born.

C   Present your ideas during your next class.

4.5 TIME TO SPEAK Every last detail

A   **Choose an event to plan from the box below.**

> a class reunion   a team-building weekend for work
> a friend's important birthday party   an evening with clients from out of town
> a weekend-long family reunion   a weekend retreat for artists and writers

B   **Think about what you need to do to host the event. Start with big-picture elements. Then list the smaller steps necessary to achieve each goal. Use your ideas to create an action plan.**

C   **Make a poster to advertise your event. Present your poster in your next class and explain your action plan.**

5.5 TIME TO SPEAK Make the case

A   **Choose the job that you think is best for you.**

> truck driver   park ranger   librarian   software developer
> teacher   sports coach   police officer   newspaper reporter

B   **Think about why the job you chose would be best for you.**

C   **Give a presentation to your class, explaining which job you chose and why that job would be best for you.**

6.5 TIME TO SPEAK Planning a surprise

A   **Think of friends or family members who deserve a fun, special surprise. Think about what kinds of things they like, what they dislike, whether they like surprises, and whether they have any fears or phobias.**

B   **Choose the surprise you think a friend or family member would like. Then ask that person whether or not he or she would actually enjoy that surprise.**

C   **In your next class, describe the surprise you chose, why you chose that surprise, and how your friend or family member react to the idea.**

Key: U = Unit.

Text

U5: Text about Lullabot. Copyright © Lullabot, Inc. Reproduced with kind permission.

Photographs

All the photographs are sourced from Getty Images.

U1: 3alexd/E+; PhonlamaiPhoto/iStock/Getty Images Plus; Vesnaandjic/E+; tickcharoen04/iStock/Getty Images Plus; metamorworks/iStock/Getty Images Plus; Hero Images; Tom Merton/OJO Images; Nazman Mizan/Moment; **U2:** NicolasMcComber/E+; pixelfit/E+; Ken Redding/Corbis; Caspar Benson; Sven Hagolani/Corbis; FatCamera/E+; vgajic/E+; **U3:** 10'000 Hours/DigitalVision; Ezra Bailey/DigitalVision; Siphotography/iStock/Getty Images Plus; kali9/E+; franckreporter/iStock/Getty Images Plus; Jack Hollingsworth/Photodisc; wynnter/E+; Bettmann; **U4:** ConstantinCornel/iStock/Getty Images Plus; Mikko Lepistö/EyeEm; Salah Mrazag/EyeEm; PhotoAlto/Antoine Arraou; RossHelen/iStock/Getty Images Plus; Hero Images; **U5:** mammuth/iStock/Getty Images Plus; Matt Walford/Cultura; Vath. Sok/500px; Ariel Skelley/DigitalVision; PeopleImages/E+; Luis Alvarez/DigitalVision; kohei_hara/E+; **U6:** Spondylolithesis/E+; Henglein and Steets/Cultura; TIMOTHY A. CLARY/AFP; Cavan Images/Cavan; Frank Bienewald/LightRocket; GlobalStock/E+.

The following photographs are sourced from other libraries.

U5: Copyright © Lullabot, Inc.; **U6:** Copyright © International Olympic Committee.

Front cover photography by Hans Neleman/The Image Bank/Getty Images Plus/Getty Images.

Typeset by emc design ltd.

Audio

Audio production by CityVox, New York.

Corpus

Development of this publication has made use of the Cambridge English Corpus (CEC). The CEC is a multi-billion word collection of contemporary spoken and written English. It includes British English, American English, and other varieties. It also includes the Cambridge Learner Corpus, the world's biggest collection of learner writing, developed in collaboration with Cambridge Assessment. Cambridge University Press uses the CEC to provide evidence about language use that helps to produce better language teaching materials. Our Evolve authors study the Corpus to see how English is really used, and to identify typical learner mistakes. This information informs the authors' selection of vocabulary, grammar items and Student's Book Corpus features such as the Accuracy Check, Register Check, and Insider English.